Copyright © 2008 by Anarda Nashai

School Girl: Poetry and Prose of a Pre and Post Adolescent

All rights reserved. Published in the United States of America.

Reproduction or translation of any part of this work beyond that permitted by section 107 or 108 of the 1976 United States Copyright Act without the permission of the copyright owner is unlawful. Requests for permissions or further information should be address to the author directly.

Library of Congress Cataloging in Publication Data:

ISBN 978-0-615-25758-7

Printed in the United States of America

Note to Readers....

First, I owe you an explanation.

While cleaning one day more recently, I came across some of my old journals, notebooks from which I would select my poems for this collection. Having found my love for not only poetry, but of the written word entirely as a fifth grader, I began writing poetry officially at the age of thirteen. Besides a few submissions for my English classes, I've had yet to share what I've written with the world. Honestly, I'll say that my fear of inadequacy kept me from doing so. Nevertheless, I feel that it's finally time for me to shelve this apprehension and attempt do what so many writers have done for me: create, share and inspire.

Now in my late twenties, I feel more of a connection with these words than when I wrote them as a child. Consequently, these feelings have kept me awake at night since finding my journals again. I've thought about this constantly and couldn't come up with any excuse or explanation to keep them hidden away. They are no longer the diaries of an often lonely but mostly excited girl, hungry for knowledge and a wonderful way of expressing herself. But still, they are just the same; feelings and thoughts that I've recorded and have kept sacred all these years.

So, I would like to thank you for taking the time to witness a huge milestone in my life. When I decided to do this, I knew that it meant opening the door to my most intimate thoughts, and I have accepted and embraced this challenge fully. Here is what I consider to be the best collection of my work: an insight into this school girl's mind. Enjoy!

I would like to dedicate this book to:

Countee Cullen, Robert Frost, Anne Sexton, and Sonia Sanchez.

Knowing you all through your work has been a precious and life-changing burden (and I mean that in the best possible way). Thank you for your examples, inspiration and company.

School Girl

Poetry and Prose of a Pre and Post Adolescent

School Girl

now that my teachers know I'm a writer
they say I'm special
…but I'm not really
i describe things with my heart and mind
compare feelings to wind and to shadows
i see people and places, eyes and hands
and form similes and stanzas
when people open their mouths to speak
i hear it for what it is to me
i mention pleasure and pain as far and as wide
as my youth will take me
if I taste or smell something sour
i will write that down and keep it forever
that's all
i'm not special
i'm a school girl…
just as silly and restless
as the rest of them.

(1994 – written at 14)

1993

at Thirteen

Reptiles, Monkeys, Seals

the gatekeeper says
"welcome"
but i hear
"we are at the zoo!"
from my classmates
….and they are all right:

first the reptiles
small lizards lick their tongues at me
are they flirting, or just hungry?
like sly bobby…like fat Richard
it's all gross either way
and the alligators
move slowly toward me
with small feet and eyes
his mouth comes open
and the glass that separates us
feels as thin as this page
i run…..

second are the monkeys
smooth hair and plump thumbs
their offspring wrapped on their backs
black noses and yellow teeth
like mean theresa and dirty tyrone
the chimps are there too
smaller, faster, dressed in sweaters
their eyes question me
"where are the bananas?"
I check my backpack
put my hand inside
cover my brown bag lunch
"nope…this one is mine!"

third, the seals
drenched and sweating to entertain us
the reflection of the sun
caught from their gray backs
they clap too loud and need our attention
like that brat mickey and that girly girl alexis
it dives in the water

splashed me in the second row
comes back up and I clap too
but it splashes me again
i stomp off to get a paper towel…

"did you all enjoy the school trip today?
my teacher holds up her hand to be heard
"yes" everyone answers
but me
i sit chewing my turkey and cheese sandwich
at the wooden picnic table
"special?" i think
"we didn't have to leave school for this!"

Gray Days

I have gray days
With no hay days
With no May days
But gray stays….

I've seen yesterdays
With my play days
With my birthdays
Most with gray clays…

I've had my says
With awful days
And angry ways
My today prays.

Me and My Singing

Me and my singing
Me and my singing
Me and my singing
Before I can try
Me and my angel
Me and my angel
Me and my angel
We look at the sky
An angel from heaven
An angel from heaven
An angel from heaven
Before I ask why
The sun has gone down
The sun has gone down
The sun has gone down
And we say goodbye.

Smiling

Glancing at the still sky
That is beautiful but gray
With my forged smile.

Rainbows

My vision today:
so vivid and clear
For a moment it seems
I am walking in beauty.

Thirsty

The waters, the waves
Appear unusually crisp
Chanting for my eye.

Hammered Down

After counting the
Nails in my face I have
Noticed a sincere grimace
This pain, your nails.

Wildlife

Through the troubled trail
In the wild midst of crazed trees
The wilderness screams….

My Perfect Sister

Your eyes are
Crossed not straight
Between the third and
Fourth molar there
Is a space...

Moon Fever

There it is!
As big as the world
As small as a pale face
There it is….

There it sits
The moon, dripping through my window
Struggling to be seen
There it sits

There it shines
Sparkles light my eyes
While its gleam lights my heart
There it shines

There it dances
And puts on a show
With all the world watching
There it dances
There it sets
Melting and fading while the sky
Is crying for it to stay,
it sets.

Lovetown

In all the years
with nurture and serenity, it is crowned
   until the ocean pulls up to Juliet's feet again
this town has burned to the ground...

Though crazy, sad messes it has aided
but this news is murder and me makes no sound
   until birds shit good luck on the devil's hideous kingdom
this town has burned to the ground.

1994

at Fourteen

Thoughts Before a Dream

Knees bent arms
Arching outward
Diving before gagging
Realizing the safety of ground
Moving water is never safe…
Diving then drowning
TRAUMATISM.

Ink in My Pen

Crimson of spontaneous
Tidal flowing outward across
To Aare
Seeing me, no eyes but ears
My brain…
Holding my red pen
Of red ink
My red smoke
Hands set a fire!

Redundancy Becomes Her

There is a
Lonely girl in
Her, nudged in the
Corner of her subconscious
"Doctor....
She is starring into
Oblivion,
Playing hopscotch
In her blue bobby socks
With her thirty year old voice
Counting the marked squares
When life becomes hard
She wants licorice and
Lollipops, ladybugs and lullabies
When life gets hard
She falls to her knees in that corner
And won't respond to her name
Doctor please tell me
Where is she?...where does she go?"

This Time, It's Black

So now
You want to know
What color
Exactly what color
I am
Well
Ask me tomorrow
Now I am
A puff of climatic smoke
And like a man
Who has lost another hard war
I am fading to black
Fading
To
Black
Ask me tomorrow
If I feel like that.

People Talk Too Much

You can greet the words
Say "hi" or "hey"
Hold them up and spread
Them thin
Thicker than thin
But don't say them
Be careful
You see…
To the poet…it's simple
Letters belong to words
With rhythm…
Rhythm to be sustained of
Lines in a page
To the poet…it's pleasure
To let your fingers
Debate and create.

Blood

Veins that run forever
Filled with the blood of my brother
Run with life and courage
Run through stone walls of ever-lasting life
Stand to let statistics crumble
Holler to let others know
That the blood from you may be theirs too:
Our blood that runs through and through.

Moon Dust

Little man tied his shoes
When he was one...
Walked with a marble
Under his thumb...
Learned hard lessons soon
As he scraped dust from the moon....
He lost his battle with sin
And that dust from the moon swept with the wind...
The little man that was put to sleep in a rocking chair
Is now an old man with a spaced stare.

Mumbo Jumbo

Cross my mind
Like wine…
Fine and genuine
Words
They run through me.

Makes my throat jump
While my brain wave thump
"chitty-bump-bump…"
Words….
They run through me

Gives me something to say
And my body a sway
Sends silence away
Words….
They run through me

They let my mouth hold
Let it hold soul
Gives me all control
Them words, they sho' run through me

Swells in my head and bursts
Finds my knowledge first
Quenches intellectual thirst
Words….chile,
They run through me.

Happiness, Sanctuary

"Oh, thank you Lord"
For my gracious mood
I am grateful to see another day
Life beats my window and smiles
I feel it's touch pass through
And I say aloud
"this is why I'm here,
To see life as I look out
To feel the light on my cheeks,
I am here to pass the night
And here to greet the morning,
I am here to think
And to be a thought
I am here to listen
Here to work and play
I exist to be
Anarda Nashai
"And Lord I am here!"
I say this with my hands
To the big cloud in the sky
I am glad to be alive
And no matter what grief comes in May

I will find a way to laugh
Yes, there is a way
To hold that air outside
And somehow
I will make
At least one person in this gray world
Laugh and hold with me
I will demand
That they too
Be happy to live.

Street Meat

Alley ways; traffic lights
Sidewalk trash; rat bites
Terrible traits; dirty feet:
The corner store smells of street meat.

Crippled cats; burning tires
Pregnant children, professional liars
Neighborhood block parties, a Motown beat:
My history smells of street meat.

Christmas lights, ginger bread
The straightening comb, my nappy head
Those evil winters, that blazing summer heat:
I welcome the stilled aroma….
A smell of street meat.

To My Best Friend

I am you
In different forms
Each day
I have since
Been drawn to you
My mind is full with you
As you erase that
Empty space from the past
I have tapped your shoulder
You have looked me in the eye
I have held you
And sometimes watched you fly away
I believe in you
I have replaced you
And you have multiplied
Oh, the confusion you've caused
My pride you have left swollen
When it calms
You leave me strong
Full of life
Full of me
I look in the mirror
And see you completely
Our kinship is obvious
To anyone that sees
To you
To the real me
I find my entire life
In you.

Uninvited

Ten year old pig tails
Clear, jelly sandals
From the classroom
Through the school gate
Friends
Fallen play yard fences
Candy store
Stepping on cracks in the sidewalk....

Then....

Young brown masculine hands
White leather covered feet
From a vacant alley way
Reaching out and pulling back
Hands
Breast
Backside
Calluses on my crying mouth
Releasing at the sound of something coming

Next....
Gravel
Piss
Terror
Confusion
A life replaced by the scales of shame.

And now....

Silence.

1995

at Fifteen

Words (A Dedication)

you are what i leave out
when letting off public steam from smooth trains
you are what stays in the back of my throat
when asked to "tell" what this life is like
you are what i use to explain
what my mouth can or will not speak or retain
you are what sleeps in my sky with the moon
(my nightlight while searching, sleeping in the dark)
you are why my dreams are wonderful and wild
you pick the light from the sun and hold it at a short mile
you are what sweeps my states of confusion
and temporary sadness to smog
you are what i need to keep tucked in my pockets
when the devil sneaks up as my shallow
you are what helps me pick up the very stubborn stones in my way
so that i will eventually get by and play
you are the motivation and satisfaction
that will hopefully, one day, allow me
to stand and shake loose my armor—
to let go a long, overdue sigh.

Diary of Little Miss Darling Girl

Oh Ma'am
It's ok
Don't worry about those
Smashed beans and
Bruised egg plants
Don't worry if they stink up the place
For me, there are always worst things to cry about
If I were seven again and
Whipped every other weekend
I would have held my little black sock
In my mouth
I wouldn't have let them see me cry
I would tell myself that those lashings
Of yours were just as harmless as the slime
Of daddy's spit in your face
When he left you with one cigarette
And his bottle of moonshine
(the aroma of both still breaking your heart)
Two million cigarettes since then
Laces with a new piece of shit
That's six feet and five inches long
(his raggedy mustache and not-so-easy charm)
Don't worry about the substance of these mistakes
You see
But please
Tell me…
Why my children won't really mature
Past twenty-three afterthoughts
And why I chase
A huge white cannon ball
Headed down the slickest
And steepest hill of my lifetime
Tell me why I chase that ball
With tap shoes and oiled hands?
You may not know this but
I am watching you
I watched you write those love letters
I watched you cry while you sliced bread
Instead of hard onions
I saw you reach down inside yourself
And find the will

To eat shit, throw it up
eat the same shit again
and die
I see your hands
For the first time in fifteen years
And well
No calluses or bruises really
Thick polish on your brown fingernails
Letting me know that you
Have hidden shame somewhere
But why, ma'am?
And why am I afraid of the bits and chips
Of the same momentous impressions
Carving onto my own aging hands?

Movement (Dedicated to Sonia Sanchez)

clear for poetic whispers
the air
be that color tonight
there is a rejuvenating stroke
through the texture of your words
familiar and comforting
...finally
an echo from some other source
than the crevices of my crowded brain
your texture
on this ten grown seventy
the thunder and lightening
i've been hearing but has stopped
since i've found you
i've heard them clear:
life is dreaming painfully, hands bleeding, eyes tightening...
gee...it's funny
i share your soprano sky
i am it's burnt black and misty blue
and like you...
my skin has been stirred
not shaken
stirred and ripped
yet to my stinging tears
i shall not awaken
so anyway...
just so you know
the color of my every hour
changes like seeds of dust in the rain
and for you
clear is tonight's gratitude
regardless of yesterday and tomorrow
thank you.

The Poet and the Sea

Instantly, the tide washes me in
After being swept away
In another wave of your
Salty, whirling mayhem
Before I can breathe
Lift my head from the sand
I see your wave at my feet again
I pound my closed fist into the wetness
"Not again!"
But still
I welcome the unpredictable routine
Even as I'm tired I know
That this feeling is only pain
And this pain never leaves me
Does not leave me
Nor ever will
But I've stayed and I'll stay
I stay, hoping that this tide will wash me in
A little easier than your last.

A Young Man Sits Down Next To Me

On a bench nailed down
To the concrete's resistance
There sat me
And my two books on philosophy
"How are you?"
He sat and inquired,
Suddenly, came all the other colors
Not reflected on the wheel...
Like pure white
Was not right
By God, he holds my kryptonite
And almost the ladder to my cooling girlhood
"Who are you and where are you from?"
Me listening and not moving
With my jaw nailed to the concrete's resistance
Looked at him and his rainbow
I looked past him--
I am thinking about his black hair in my palms
I am thinking about his broad shoulders in my arms
I am seeing my swollen hands and fat arms
I am seeing my awkward shadow with Honeycut's crown
...his solid trunk and soothing smile
...my blotched skin and crooked calves
What would he think if I said:
My soul is old
And my feelings too preoccupied
To engage you with sidewalk conversation
And what would his momma think?
She would curse me to her distant relatives
She would beg you to have lunch once more
With her neighbor's beautiful daughter
And what of your other admirers?
They will pull you from the laughing stock
Then wait for me to turn my head
And flick lit matches into your lap
No, I can't compete
With their made faces
I am old
With ink stains in my nails
And in this big homely dress
With delicate yellow flowers.

From a Relic

I am survived to be loved
I just want to breathe deep
Brought back from my sleep.

A Rock and A Nickel

An old woman asked me one day:
"What do you know little girl?"
And with a nickel in one hand
And a rock in the other I said:
"I know that my nickel is silver,
And my rock is white,
And if I squeeze them together
I could crush them at once
And buy soul food for you tonight!"
She looked at me before she laughed
She smoothed my pony tail down my back and said:
"Baby girl, you still a chile
And your words sound absurd
But if I were still little
And loved fairy tales
It would be the most wonderful idea
I ever heard."
So I skipped away then
And now I wonder what her question really meant
Then it occurred to me to look into my hands
To figure out where my rock and nickel went.

Days of Our Lives

Lives to be stolen
Hearts to be broken
Love stays unspoken
….these are the days.

Jazz

I am sitting and waiting for love
When it taps me on the shoulder
And startles my ignorant waiting awake
Waiting for that love
Not knowing it was all taboo
I listen to love while I wait
Love that is as precious as life
And I am surprised that it loves me too
Wanting love so badly it's crazy
And it seemed twice as meaningful before tonight
And I finally know that love I've searched for
And can bask in my love at first sight.

Untitled

It's like your smile
Opens up to me
It unravels and
Poses for me
And how I want
You picture
But you are not
Still for me
Oh, Lord
What color
Is my broken heart
The center of my universe:
"I will stand forever to see you…
Oh, the color of my love."

True Impromptu

Up in the air
With my toes arched downward
The flies on the tree are ready
To watch my tranquil sweat
Green with envy at
The bumblebee's two step
I let by braids fly
And sounds from my teeth
Let go
...and you still can't believe
That I used to dance?

Self-Esteem

Tomorrow
While I am among
The daylight
I would like to count
The spaces between the migrating clouds
But today
And the day before that
The sturdy soil
That secretes the grass
Knows and remembers
My constant admiration
I search between the green blades:
Where is my mother's beautiful daughter?

Another Innovation

If I were cursed
With the potential to be perfect
I would reject, with one look
Today's existing pigments
That make me the architect
Of thick stone men
I would insist that
I be given the chance to
Mix my own intrinsic formula
To be the creator
I wouldn't be a judge
But a creator
Of self empowerment.

How She Dances

Dwelling in her lyrical habitat
Surrounded by her holy prose
The poet spins….

A Tribute to the Cold

A mere gasp with afflictions
Full of harrowing flows of susceptibility
Walking intrepidly through these psyched roads
I do not write love songs.

Hope Has a Place

Crying on holey tissues
Staring with blood shot eyes at heaven
Here's a welcome with my gratitude…
You have found a way in.

Sadness

The color of this year's
Emotional implosion?
It lay an ill-marked gift box
Left on my un-lit porch
My hot hands burn more
As I rip its flaps and dig for the contents:
Let it be chronic numbness....

The Color of Smothering

The suffocation of blackness
Between this earth and mars
Past hour glass sand is unknown
Doesn't matter though
I have smeared clouds with tact
I continue to laugh with the stars
…the bluest blue before skies
The offering of that blackness
Before magic and tars.

Frightening Times

Here I am again
Swept with the strong current
A strictness of disappointment
The claws of its unavoidable presence
Squeezes my tired flesh
Until I give in
And bleed
Burns the hell out of a heart
That is full and ready to burst
Disappointments seem to grown on those
That are unaccounted for
And they fester
My hands grown sick
Of wiping tears of acid
That eat at my disappointed face
I look like a disappointed girl
I reek of disappointment through perfume…
Here are the times that frighten me most of all.

Grim Reaper

Cold heart
Burning skin
No mercy
For man's sin
Screams and cries
A swollen throat
Here comes hell
In a long, black coat.

My Reality

Soon smoothed across
Paper and
Scooped for sensibility
Scrapped past it's
Spoken vibrations
Watched while
Wind whimpers,
Wide awake when
Willows want war,
Apparently ample for
Arrogant admirers to kiss.

Sufferance

I remember
I talked to you…
You spit back
A loose baby tooth
Damn! That was cold….

I remember
I sang to you
You plugged your ears
And sang back in silence
I am quiet since then…

I remember
I danced for your
You shut your eye
And turned your head
That shadow in the corner is now mine

I remember
I cried to you…
You showed me to be humorous
And shook you head this time
Now I am tall and thick

I remember
I bled for you
And you looked down at me, walked away
I stay frozen in that blood
Otherwise, a dead girl walking.

1996

at Sixteen

Untitled

That red line
Across the moon
Has dissolved
To have the glow of one side
Confused with the
Fairness of the other
Everybody sees this
And nobody sees the same
So when I point out the line
And look to compare my answers
Who can I ask?
To stop and question these "bodies"
Would be a disaster
And so formed is
A question of nature
It lay stationed on my
Stubborn idealism
I am announced today:
Another young victim of cynicism.

No Love on Stage, Not Yet

You see
The young poet is overworked
Overlooked unjustly

And I myself am a traitor
I absolutely understand why…

Who could imagine
A youngster's audacity
Someone whose eyes
Have only touched
But a few of those
Free-flying white summer "flurries"
…whose eyes have only pissed
But a few blood-stained tears
Unwrapped by inexperience
That actually scrape and burn
With this lesson not yet learned:
Things fall apart and fly away….

Who would believe that "this" poet
Was capable of holding thousands of swords
In their free-styled open sores

And to my own questions I say:
I do
And I will
I will hold my chest
And squint my eyes
In the black lit room
I will continue to dwell in this room
With Holiday, and with Hugo, and with Fanon
Prop myself on biology and chemistry books
Lean forward to the journal
And press my ears to the
Plainness of my page
I will listen to everything it tells me
For years and years and years
With hopes to earn a place
In the most spectacular
Of all lyrical archives

Yes, my sixteen will grow seventy
In just a short while

You'll see.

Discouraged

Swindling in my face
Like dust through a bike ride
Like mud that travels
And lives with the wind
Only to be known as
Dry itching sand
Hard on sensitive ears
Blasting behind red eyes:
Discouragement
Overflows in a cup
Of boiling unhappiness
Church-goers do not see this
They look at my blank face
And praise me for being so self-aware
They come with a cursive agenda
And thus are too easy to fool
Little do they know
That the dust that swindles is annoying…
That the nuisance of it all is stinging
…and that this discouraging mood is winning
…little do they know
That their wonderful play days
Are in my history books
And that these times are combined
Into the devil's stage play
Little do they know how hard it will get
To keep tasteful wine
Flowing form a vineyard
That is constantly interrupted
The chaos is rough and not appreciated
Discouraged…
Like the sun that tempts freezing Alaska
Discouraged….
Like me:
Searching for cotton candy trees
Only to find the sweetness
Melting into life's lakes and seas…
Discouraged.

Self-Righteous Loner

You've found that you have another mouth to tame
To love me, to hate me…it's all the same
And here is something else you'll be quick to call lame
"When your sand finds my ocean
To make the shore
My role in this creation
Will tap your soul at the core
And say
I've never stood with armies
I've stood alone
I stand
Try and move me if you can!

Trust

A cure vs. a plague
Vague of decent description
This cure
With no casualty of evil
Its armor lives in rusting seas
With cleaver sharks to protect
My life from there after waving to going ships
Watching stars engulfed by murderous skies
Of greed and of power and of other musty things
…and here, my life in the balance hung
Devoured by the later mentioned earlier
Run finally from brute and havoc's dust
With my fate instills a dangerous mistrust
And so, *Fair Naïveté*, from you I go
Through my genetic map I hence with my right
To never kneel, cry or kiss you goodbye
And would rather burn in hell if I must.

With Sleep Comes Temptation, With Winter Comes Death

Who sleeps in a clear sky
And longs for blue fantasies
And maroon nightmares
….lies in the arms of chocolate, milk
Of caramel and coffee
Just to mention the taste of sweets?
It is for comparison's sake that they are not made bitter
For the same that it is not mentioned
When the sweet turns over, flat sided
On the owls great and nightly tongue
When will these shivering birds decide
To flock naturally to the south's safety in December?
Why do they stay to face pleasure's refute?
To wallow in the death of last year's caress?

I Don't Write Love Poems

I don't suppose that August
Would cradle my loneliness
Tonight or the night after

And I don't look forward
To August in my head
When I am counting strains
Of grass in my dreams
I know that August will not come
From blue and white
To green and agony

August
Painted perfectly along
The surface of my womanhood
Does not hear the pit of me
When I cry
Looks straight past this
And into my eye

I doubt if August can allow
The song of my well-oiled heart
To encourage admiration
August seeks nothing
But for my cracked mask
To be restricted to comedy

Needless to say
That warm signs August today
But I've opened the door
To get my tan one day
And so brute is the storm
That stings me this way
Yes
To keep my hands riddled with ink
And my mind focused on sought after stars
And the ones I've missed:
August has found a way.

Life is Dreaming Painfully

Tightly….
I have held on to my sadness
Adjusting to the acceptance
Of disappointment
Slowly…

If only
I could curb the eagerness
Of my young, clumsy hands
Be that as I dream….
Never…

Quietly
I aid the sores of worn feet
Familiar to all corners of hell
But ailments of tomorrow
Eventually.

History Brings Tears

Days of no more
Keep us apart
With a generous memory box
Full of glass and wood:
Glittering and splintering
They pull my thoughts
 To that energetic tike
Running along with a kite
And tomorrow's mirror
I run through
The thunder and lightning with it
I'm still here
Before I mention the starved bats
That have held me in their bosoms
Know that my health and the fair weather
Was the Lords' blessing
Since I was frail and allergic to everything
A blessing indeed
To lil ole me
though my pre-mature down-ness
Is diagnosed far too late:
An example of life's clutch on the speechless

So I lay down those days
Of my past
I am so very sorry
That I leave these things with you…
For your being history
Keeps us apart.

A Minor Struggle

Help me
With ears of brail
So that my eyes
No longer feel
Drawn lips that spit
Words to draw blood…
Strings of tight wire
Through my stiffened air…
For the love of rust
That stretches inside
Help me.

Help me
And my life
That stays together
Only with man-made adhesives to wear
Only with this magic mirror to spare
Live me long
So that "life" can
Honestly say he knows me there
For the love of life
That pain cannot bear
Help me!

Rapture

Loose after fire holds its hand
Full with gospel and glory
Credited with hopelessness and despair
Puzzled with numbed skeletons
And loud echoes through dead hair
Ripped from lonely vagabonds
Floating to livelihood here and there
Leaving plain queens to die alone
With a golden throne to care.

Sunshine and Moonlight

Life after shiny sand
Turn to dirt
…is not considered soil anymore
…only filth that gives a rash

Time after it's wasted
Rolls over like a hog after killing time
…it cannot be brought back to life
…I can only be eaten or buried

Stories from back then
Believed and are begged to be tried
…you can only look at the face of the past
…and know that you will ball the same way, some day

Hands that only belong
To hold a paint brush in one hand
And a almanac in the other
…these hands that are clean and wipe tears

It goes down and comes up just the same:
Creativity brings it all back to a shine.

If You Were Ignorant and I Was a Teacher

who is to say
that ignorance doesn't have a reason?
ignorance
lives and breathes
to figure "reason" out
it lives freely
(does not pay taxes or need shelter from weather)
but where do you send it
when you say "go home!"
and he resides in YOU?
for where is the comfort
in thinking this concept through:
the fact that ignorance is sharing a roof with you!

who is to say
that ignorance doesn't have a reason?
for its because of ignorance
my quest is for knowledge
(the popular turtle that it is...)
it's purpose
is to give life plenty of examples
of tragedy and hope...
of flimsy paper, or melting plastic
(both completely unreliable, but are our only choices)

for if ignorance where a tree
and I were the soil
how many raindrops would the sky save
so that its seeds wouldn't grow or spoil
for we are all trinkets
in this tree's closet
and we choose everyday
which kind of trinkets we will be:
of costume or of dynasty (?)
of peace or of travesty (?)
would we choose calmly or hostilely (?)
...and if you look closely at your history, see
we trinkets are held down by ignorance
and not gravity...

who is to say

that ignorance doesn't have a solution?
we read our books, ponder, then report
with our ignorance masked by so-called "intelligence"
...the mache derived from ignorant sources

...for if ignorance were a tunnel
and your conscience a train...
besides yourself and the road chosen
your derailment has no one else to blame...
for having a head on your shoulders
and being "smart" are not at all the same:
it's HUNGRY ignorance
and it's leech on our minds
that has no shame.

Truth...or Dare?

"...and here is to embellishment...
whose very essence can seem
the relic of reward!"
if when you read this
with your lips pursed with epiphany
your forehead constricted in seriousness
pulling your neck steadily in agreement....
if THIS is your philosophy
when i ask you for the truth:
then you're a fucking liar...
NO EXCEPTIONS!!!

The Advantage of Being Grape Juice

when you swallowed his warm words
(to both you and me, vibrations of indubitable masculinity)
and drew them in with a promise to GOD:
"If you were to let me have him, oh Father
to count the grey spurs on my eighty-year-old temples
i would (blah, blah, blah)...
in Jesus name
Amen!"
when you lost yourself in his starlit courtship
and the gentleness of his hand
cruising the vulnerability of your hot-flashing skin
when his aura turned your child-like afternoons
into hard, naughty dusks
you were happier
counting your new silvers dollars
from those now worthless quarters
(they were worthless, aye?)
and your search was over....

when he spoke of me
(and i'm sure he did)
he must have "mistaken satin from silk" he said
he told you that in me
he had discovered how tight caterpillars
gave him a grave distaste for grape juice
and had insisted that your silken existence
had him parched for thick, red wine
when he had you gussy up your face
with post-adolescent pinks
and come down to his town fairs
across his wide bayou by ferry
when he stole your knee-length dresses
and had you mock a downed,
high-split wearing co-ed from Uni-V
when i saw you skipping merrily to the play yard
from your favored boardroom
i opened my opinion
stretched it's clumped-ness into curiosity
and poured expeditiously
...but quietly...

maybe i shouldn't have been...so satisfied
with your cheery passing...
to see your face a brand new shade of joy
and maybe i should have listened up and loosed his wine
so that your pillow wouldn't be stained
with those tastes he leaves behind
for through you it is proven
that loosened autumn leaves
blow whisk fully around and around by nature's cruelty
until a pausing summer breeze interrupts
to end the appropriate violence
and though you are a most splendid leaf--
the unjust laws of nature intrudes without mercy
and stays forever unchanged
no matter how much you cry
or are hurt by it all
nevertheless it was forced onto you
by your mother and mine:
"FALLING IN LOVE is way too easy to do..."
i'll bet a million bucks that even now
you'll either accept or reject
these two cents on this sincere page
and won't really weigh in my meaning
yep...you'll bite the dust with the rest
my dear, I SHOULD HAVE WARNED YOU
when he moaned his first hello...
but i'm merely fresh grape juice:
too sweet and immature
to be the deliverer of bad news.

1997

at Seventeen

When a Teenage Poet Writes of a Lover's Love

When our war takes a spotlight
…and when our feelings take their part
Under the light we feel vulnerable and exposed
And we wait for apologies from the invading audience
…as they witness the corruption of our vacant hearts
No standing ovations are allowed when we finish
And where are the stems of roses
And wide air kisses?

But still, when we warriors come home
To see that these civilians are still there
We sure don't care about plays and such
Instead we watch the losing end of the war
In homage of heroes who never existed to start
Guns, Cannons, berets…those stupid stage plays
We sit and eat and play in the mud pits
And wait for the gun smoke to clear.

If Heaven Is Waiting (For Countee Cullen)

There are hurdles in your eye
Long, deep inset in your eye
Waiting to comfort my intrusion
(Not refuse, but comfort…just like I said)
There is a wisdom on your fingertips
Sliding, slick and embedded in your fingertips
And I wouldn't mind a smack from you
Rub my eyes, ears, and sore heart
Give me a road that's clear and dry
It will lead to my everlasting peace
Yes, there is comfort here:
One shaded land rock
After swimming in summer's
Steamed and muddy lake:
There is heaven in your eye.

On Being Human

Reminiscent moments
Curving all aspects of
Today's romantic feeling
Is proven by my willful past
To be long overdue
And is welcomed
When my mind is clear
Candle-lit visions
Are not to describe
Lovers entwined
But to celebrate something more
Something that is rarely allowed in
That has slept on the curb
With all that is physical in me
A secret sigh
Help up for literature to see:
For I do have a heart
That is alive and red
Under my cruel rap of poetry
Ok…so I'm human (there, I said it!)
So, for those who love romance?
Record this remarkable prose
I'm afraid there aren't too many more of those.

Shit in a Cornfield on a Stifling Afternoon

Clinging flies clash with my reaction
To an agitating cloud that pitifully bellows
After the aroma hits the hot air
Its stench ain't mellow

Viewing the sun through such
Ever so dull from its traditional yellow
I am waiting for its marinating
Mounting to settle

I've read a book
And I do not agree with its contents
(Yes, I'm here again, and comparing it to shit)

Lavish avenues gone,
Normal atmosphere has burned
Lonely conquests to travel
Evil lessons to learn

Mortal attitudes stay adjusted
Like that state of chaos we've earned
On a hot day in a cornfield
That shit has returned.

A Hard Kill For Gratitude Tonight

My hand and the wind:
Mildly coinciding on bare or gloved fingers
Inevitably in the winter's bust,
Take a blue sky with bright clouds:
Me
Actually surrendering to the company of such
It's daylight from which night owls escape
Loving my thoughts and imagination
My fingerprints and concentration.

A Proposal from Grace

A mind that is full
With the weeping and clouded view
Of hands meant to stay
Black and plain
Raises them up to her face
And kisses them the same
As if she stood before an alter
With a white dress
And virtuous scripture
OH Yes…she does marvel
And she loves.

When I Don't Write Anything in Weeks (I think I am tired....)

How different the streets seem
Not two but twenty lanes
All their inhabitants flowing
Forth against my grains
My nose gets wider and wider
And I try to dodge them "thangs"
My feet they never seem tired
Dear God:
My seventeen year old feet won't
Stop dodging
But my mind:
"Damn!!! Where is the curb?"
All I see is the street
ALL I SEE IS THE STREET
The same street I piss in:
Two lanes then
Twenty lanes now.

A Day in the Park

Transcendentalism
Is gone, burned to ashes
(we seem to only help ourselves)
I walk in
Creep though a world of chaos
But I refuse to see evil
Destructive people
(disrespect and damnation)
Through the deeds
Of my brothers and sisters
Who seem unable to be changed
But they breathe and need water the same as me.
True change takes place
In the womb and tomb they say
I watch different faces
Painted with hostility and pain
(I see love taking over,
Love in every wrinkle of their faces):

When she stands with blood on her hands;
The blood of a man or child
I see love for malice
It outranks that of brotherhood
In her mind
I see love on her hands.

When he squeals words
He translates from Satan's castle
I see love for words is all
Love for symbols that sting
His throat as well…
His love of affliction.

Some words are creamy and white
She screams words considered pure
For love of lust
She clings to the image
Of American man
With her arms open to fire and ice
"Love" takes part for her sanity.

When his personal war is undone
His trunk links the tail
of the other soldiers to fight
Love is his substitute for fear
Stale actions for cowardice
For a country with a foundation of upright nails
Love is his excuse to fight and die.

There are periods of long gone wealth
She sells everything in sight
Her love for living is her ground
She stays and lives with money
But dies, her children die
For the love of living, she is dead.

He keeps a world of pretty women
Sees beauty at her face and body
(for love for gorgeous chemistry
His eyes crack with attractiveness
For love of radiance, he puts love aside
A house of trophies in disguise.

The hands of holy women
Caress a picture of Jesus and of Jerusalem
Their love of faith has taken over
The women don't own their lives
And are content with their blood and air
Faith alone is the love of their lives.

His body gives away to the world
He cannot function in human eyes
Health is his love and his vision
He settles; he gives up
Draws from the faith of the holy women
His love of health is all, but he loves.

So, we are all magnets of this thing you see
Seen past our human goggles felt without our covered hands
We see and feel something no matter our perspective
It is our third eye that will make the good or evil
…but to me, on that day in the park
The love is always there.

Painful Admission (Today's color…and tomorrows)

I will finally say this to the world. Didn't think it would be so soon…only seventeen wax-filled tears from eyes that have grown closer to an unchanged moon. I will say this now, even without right, even if my eyes are still a bright white, my tongue--still an angry red. And again with only seventeen tastes of distastes. I will say this…and I won't mention that it was not mentioned to me. One day, I just looked down past my chest, torso and feet and there was the laceration. And then suddenly it began to ooze the truth. I will make this declaration, even though it's not always on the tip of my mind pointing against the grain of everyone else's reality. Actually, it is grainy, salty, bitter: so full of bitterness…seventeen years worth. Truly, the admission of this is so against me. I'm not one to give in, and I don't usually explain my eccentricities but I will make this point:

I am not happy
I am not sad
I am not satisfied
Now days…let me see:
I'm empty but struggling
In a chokehold of my youth
My maturity
And whatever else
It all trickles away at ambitions time
And tomorrows color
Is all so very tricky:
Shades of blue that end up to me
A tunnel of dull silver
And me, a mere monger
Employed by my dreams and nightmares
Love's gate is not seen in the distance
Well…
Not love for anything other
Than a mangling, golden gate anyway.

www.ingramcontent.com/pod-product-compliance
Lightning Source LLC
LaVergne TN
LVHW011429080426
835512LV00005B/340